192 71045

D0471134

Discovering

JELLYFISH

Miranda MacQuitty

The Bookwright Press
New York · 1989

Discovering Nature

First published in the
United States in 1989 by
The Bookwright Press
387 Park Avenue South
New York, NY 10016

First published in 1989 by
Wayland (Publishers) Limited
61 Western Road, Hove
East Sussex BN3 1JD, England

© Copyright 1989 Wayland (Publishers) Limited

Library of Congress Cataloging-in-Publication Data

Typeset by DP Press Ltd., Sevenoaks, Kent
Printed in Italy by Sagdos S.p.A., Milan

WM
9
593.7
Mac
11.90

MacQuitty, Miranda.
    Discovering jellyfish / by Miranda MacQuitty.
        p. cm. — (Discovering nature)
    Bibliography: p.
    Includes index.
    Summary: Introduces the jellyfish family, whose members
include jellyfish, sea anemones, sea firs, coral, and hydras.
    ISBN 0–531–18281–9
    1. Jellyfishes — Juvenile literature. [1. Jellyfishes. 2.
Coelenterates.] I. Title. II. Series.
QL377.S4M23   1989
593.7 — dc19   89–625
                                                                CIP
                                                                AC

Cover *This jellyfish likes to drift in the sea.*
Frontispiece *A warm-water jellyfish from the Great Barrier Reef.*

WHITE MOUNTAIN LIBRARY
Sweetwater County Library System
Rock Springs, Wyoming

Contents

1
Introducing Jellyfish

This is a jellyfish stage of a sea fir that lives off the coast of Australia.

Jellyfish and Their Relatives

Jellyfish are animals that drift in the sea. They have no bones or hard skeletons and their bodies are like jelly. People are often frightened of jellyfish because they can sting. Jellyfish are beautiful creatures to look at under water, and harmless as long as you do not touch them.

Perhaps more beautiful still are sea anemones and corals, which belong to the same group of animals as jellyfish. This group is called **Coelenterates**, which means "hollow gut." Jellyfish, sea anemones and corals all have bag-like bodies with one opening through which they feed and pass out wastes.

Unlike jellyfish, sea anemones and corals are stuck onto rocks. Sea anemones are soft like jellyfish, whereas many corals have hard skeletons. Some kinds of corals grow to form reefs, which can be as hard

Above left *Sea anemones are often found on the seashore. These colorful red waratah anemones are found along the coast of Australia.*

Above right *The hard skeletons of these Red Sea corals form part of a reef. Corals grow well in tropical seas where the water is warm and clear.*

as rocks.

Sea firs also belong to the Coelenterates. They grow on rocks and seaweed and look more like delicate plants than animals. Some relatives of sea firs, such as tiny hydras, live in lakes and streams.

All members of the Coelenterates have stinging tentacles. Each sting is coiled up inside a tiny cell in the tentacle. Stinging tentacles are used to catch food and to protect jellyfish and their relatives from animals that try to eat them. People in swimming may be stung if they brush up against the tentacles of a jellyfish.

What Jellyfish and Sea Anemones Look Like

You may think jellyfish and sea anemones look very different, but they all come in two basic forms. One form is like a floating bell, with the opening, or mouth, surrounded by tentacles. This is called a **medusa**. The other form is like an upside-down bell, with the tentacles and mouth facing upward and the base stuck to a rock. This form is called a **polyp**.

Jellyfish are medusas, the floating bell form. Most jellyfish range in size from 2 centimeters to about 40 centimeters (¾ in–16 in) across the body. There are some very large kinds of jellyfish whose bodies are over 2 meters (6½ft) across. Besides the tentacles, jellyfish have four frilly arms that hang down from the rim of the body opening. These help the jellyfish to feed.

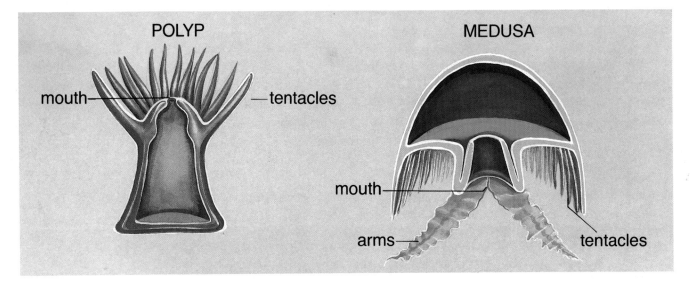

POLYP

mouth — tentacles

MEDUSA

mouth

arms

tentacles

Jellyfish swim by pulsating the rims of their bell-shaped bodies. To swim toward the surface of the sea, jellyfish contract the muscles around the body, forcing water out and propelling themselves upward. They are also moved along by currents.

Sea anemones are polyps, the form whose bases are stuck onto rocks. Some kinds of sea anemones are solitary, which means they live by themselves. Other kinds live side by side in small groups. Sea anemones range in size from about 1 centimeter to 1 meter (½ in–3 ft) across.

Sea anemones can stretch and contract their bodies, but they usually stay attached to rocks by the sucker on the base of the body. Sometimes an anemone moves by gliding along a rock surface on its sucker. One kind of sea anemone can swim by bending its body back and forth. It does this to escape being eaten by a starfish.

A jellyfish trailing its frilly arms.

Beadlet anemones can be red, green or spotted like a strawberry.

What Sea Firs Look Like

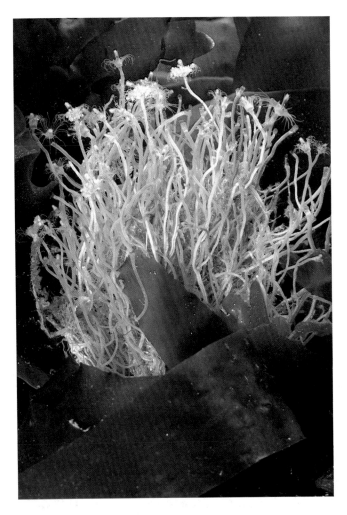

Sea firs are small, fuzzy plant-like animals that grow on rocks, seaweed, shells and pier pilings. They are anchored to these surfaces by root-like structures. Branches like those of a tree grow from the sea fir's "roots." On the branches are small polyps, which look like little flowers. Each polyp is a separate individual, so a sea fir is really a group of animals that live together as a **colony**. The sea fir's polyps do different tasks. Some are responsible for catching food, some for defending the colony, and others for reproduction.

The Portuguese man-of-war and by-the-wind sailor look like jellyfish but are more closely related to sea firs. They have balloon-like floats with a series of polyps hanging down. They live at the ocean's surface, where they are buffeted by the wind and waves.

Sea firs look more like plants than animals. This kind lives in shallow rockpools and in deeper water.

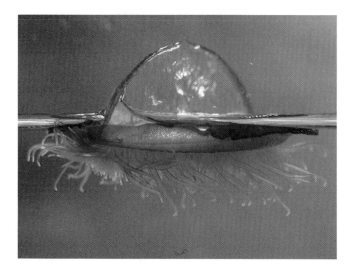

Left *A by-the-wind sailor floats along on the surface of the ocean. When the wind blows, it is propelled along by its sail. The feeding polyps stay beneath the surface of the water.*

Below *This beautiful porpita, a relative of the sea fir, looks like a little star-burst as it drifts along on the ocean currents. Its polyps hang down below its saucer-shaped float.*

The porpita is another relative of the sea fir. It also has a float to keep it at the surface of the sea. The porpita is only about 2 centimeters (¾ in) across, and the by-the-wind sailor is not much bigger, whereas the Portuguese man-of-war can be up to 30 centimeters (12 in) across.

The hydra is a freshwater relative of the sea fir. It is a solitary animal with only one polyp, which is less than a centimeter (½ in) in length.

What Corals Look Like

Most corals are colonial animals consisting of thousands of tiny polyps living together. Each polyp is only a few millimeters across and is usually encased by its own skeleton of hard limestone. The entire hard skeleton is covered by a sheet of living coral

This coral is called a brain coral because it looks like a human brain.

tissue, which connects each polyp to the one next to it. Coral polyps may be tiny, but together they form massive reefs. Some reefs are hundreds of miles long.

Corals grow in a great variety of shapes. Some, such as elkhorn and staghorn corals, are branched, while others, such as brain corals, form rounded masses. These rounded corals are also made up of tiny polyps. Mushroom corals are unusual in that they are solitary polyps that grow to about 50 centimeters (20 in) across.

In some kinds of corals, the polyps grow around a central rod-like skeleton instead of being enclosed in little cups. Sea fans grow like this, and so does the precious red coral from which jewelry is made.

Soft corals do not have hard skeletons, but tiny needles of hard material called **spicules**. These corals grow in rubbery masses. One type of

A sea fan grows with its large, flat surface spread out, so that it can filter food particles out of the water.

soft coral grows with finger-like projections and is known as dead man's fingers. This coral can grow in the cool waters around Europe. Sea pens are another kind of soft coral. They are called pens because they look like the feather quills that people once used to write with.

Origins and Relatives

Jellyfish, sea anemones and corals are simple animals that **evolved** a long time ago. Some impressions of jellyfish have been found in rocks 650 million years old. Old remains of corals are far more abundant because their hard skeletons are preserved much better than the soft bodies of jellyfish. Preserved skeletons of animals and impressions left in old

The coral fossil shown here is over 300 million years old. There are more than 6,000 types of coral fossils.

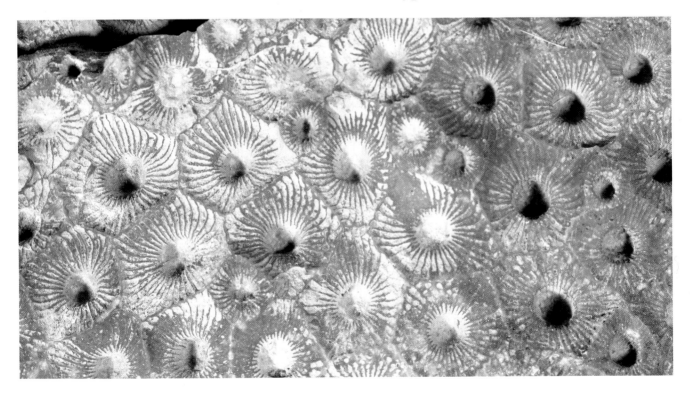

rocks are called **fossils**. There are more than 6,000 different kinds of fossil corals.

The closest relatives of jellyfish are the comb jellies. These animals are also jelly-like creatures that live in the sea. They are similar to jellyfish as they have only one opening to the body. But unlike jellyfish, they have special rows of minute hair-like projections called **cilia**. These form rows of combs, which propel the comb jellies along. As the combs beat back and forth they catch the light and appear as all the colors of the rainbow. Even at night, comb jellies look pretty as they emit light. Flashes of light pass along the comb rows. Some comb jellies have long, sticky tentacles that they use to trap food. Most comb jellies that drift along in the currents are round or oval in shape, while those that creep along the bottom are flat.

This comb jelly is called a sea gooseberry.

WHITE MOUNTAIN LIBRARY
Sweetwater County Library System
Rock Springs, Wyoming

2
Where Jellyfish Live

Purple stingers are usually found in ocean waters, but they sometimes drift inshore with the currents.

Jellyfish in the Sea

Jellyfish are found in seas and oceans all around the world. Most are found around the coasts. Swarms of jellyfish often occur in coastal waters at certain times of the year. They are frequently washed inshore and can be seen in harbors and bays. Some become stranded on the beach. Here the jellyfish soon dry out and die. Jellyfish may also be trapped in rockpools, which are good places to see them up close. You should be careful not to pick up a jellyfish in case it has a powerful sting.

Many jellyfish float in the surface waters. The common jellyfish is found in almost every sea and ocean. It is known by different names in different parts of the world. In the United States it is called a moon jelly. One kind of jellyfish, called *Cassiopeia*, floats upside down, with its tentacles

Above *The* Cassiopeia *spends much of its time upside down on the sea bottom. It is shown here swimming along.*

Left *The common jellyfish is often seen floating in sheltered harbors.*

facing upward, near the sea bottom. When this jellyfish wants to swim it flips over the right way up and contracts the edge of its bell-shaped body. Some kinds of jellyfish are found in deeper water, at depths of about 1,000 meters (3,300 ft).

Sea Anemones on the Shore and in the Sea

Sea anemones are found on the seashore in rockpools and on the undersides of rocks, where it stays damp even when the tide is out. Beadlet anemones prevent themselves from drying out at low tide by withdrawing their tentacles and contracting their bodies. In this position they look like small red blobs. When the tide comes in they open up again, ready to feed. Some seashore anemones cover their body columns with pebbles and bits of shells so that they are hard to see. If you poke them, they squirt out water. You soon know when you have found an anemone.

Some sea anemones, such as snakelocks anemones, cannot withdraw their tentacles, so they live on the bottom in rockpools that do not dry out. Other kinds of anemones are found in deeper water. They grow on any hard surface, such as rocks and pilings. Some kinds of sea anemones even live on the bottom in the deepest parts of the sea, about 10,000 meters (33,000 ft) down. Giant sea anemones are found on coral reefs.

Left *When out of the water, beadlet anemones withdraw their tentacles and contract their bodies.*

A few kinds of sea anemones burrow in mud and sand at the bottom of the sea. They have long, thin worm-like bodies, which they keep buried, showing only their tentacles above the surface of the

These burrowing anemones make tubes in which to live.

sediment. Unlike rock-dwelling sea anemones, they lack a sucker on the base of the body.

Tropical Corals

Most corals grow in tropical seas where the water is warm and clear. Reef-building corals grow only in sunlit waters because they depend for some of their food on tiny plants, called **algae**, that live inside the corals. Like all plants, the algae need light to make food. These algae grow best in

The largest coral reef in the world – Australia's Great Barrier Reef.

seawater warmer than 20°C (68°F). Reef-building corals do not grow in cooler waters or at depths greater than 70 meters (230 ft), where there is not enough light. Nor do they grow in water that is made murky by muddy rivers emptying into the sea.

There are three kinds of reefs. Fringing reefs grow at the edges of rocky shores. Barrier reefs grow farther offshore, with a lagoon separating the reef from the shore. **Atolls** are reefs that grow on the tops of old **volcanoes** that have submerged beneath the sea.

The largest barrier reef is the Great Barrier Reef off the coast of Australia. It is 1,930 kilometers (1,200 mi) long, and the lagoon that separates the reef from the mainland is about 16 to 240 kilometers (10–150 mi) wide.

Some kinds of corals are found in cooler waters; these do not form reefs. Among the corals living in cooler

The dead man's fingers is a type of soft coral found in cool waters. It is a solitary coral that does not form into reefs. The dead man's fingers has hundreds of little feeding polyps, which it will withdraw if it is disturbed.

waters are some soft corals, like dead man's fingers and the pretty little cup corals, which are solitary polyps encased in their own individual limestone cups.

A group of hydras attached to a twig. Their outstretched tentacles are ready to catch food.

In Fresh Water

Hydras are common animals that live in lakes, ponds and streams. Rather like sea anemones, they are polyps. A hydra has a simple, long-shaped body with the mouth and tentacles at one end. Hydras grow on waterweeds, stones and other surfaces, sticking on with a glue-like substance produced by their disk-shaped bases. Hydras are smaller than the length of your fingernail, so to see them clearly you need a magnifying glass.

Hydras are bright green because they have tiny plants, called algae, living inside them. The algae give the hydras some food and, in return, have a place to live. They also receive certain nutrients that help them grow. When a hydra wishes to feed, it stretches out its tentacles. But if it is disturbed, a hydra draws its tentacles and body into a small blob, making itself almost invisible.

To move from place to place, a hydra does somersaults. It bends over and holds on to the surface with its tentacles, detaching its base as it does so. Then it bends over again, reattaching its base and freeing its tentacles to stand upright.

A few kinds of jellyfish live in fresh water but most are sea creatures.

Right *This hydra has caught a tiny shrimp-like creature.*

The hydra moves by doing a somersault

3
Staying Alive

This beadlet anemone is feeding on a large prawn it has caught.

Feeding

Jellyfish and their close relatives all feed on small animals they catch with their stinging tentacles. Each sting is released from a tiny cell. There are several kinds of stings. Some are like miniature harpoons with barbs on the end that inject poison to paralyze the prey. Some jellyfish have sticky harpoons, and others wrap their harpoons around the **prey** to trap it.

Jellyfish do not chase their prey; they wait for small animals to swim or drift into their tentacles. Their prey includes a wide range of small animals that drift in the currents. These are called **plankton**. Jellyfish also eat small fish. The common jellyfish captures prey underneath its bell-shaped body as it sinks. It uses its arms to collect the food and channel it into its mouth.

Sea anemones feed only when

submerged in seawater. Some catch small animals, such as shrimp and fish, with their tentacles, which then push the food into the mouth. Bits of undigested food, such as a shrimp's skeleton, are passed out through the mouth. Sea anemones with sticky tentacles feed on bits of food and small animals floating in the sea.

Reef-building corals have hundreds of tiny polyps that feed on small particles of food in the water. They also feed on the algae that live inside the coral.

Sea firs and Portuguese men-of-war have special feeding polyps that catch food for the rest of the colony.

A Portuguese man-of-war has caught a small fish with its stinging tentacles.

Friends

Many kinds of jellyfish protect small fish. These fish are not trapped by the jellyfish's stinging tentacles. Instead, they shelter among the tentacles, protected from larger fish that might attack them.

Sea anemones also give shelter to clown fish. This brightly colored fish is not stung by the anemone's stinging tentacles, probably because it has a protective slimy coat. The clown fish

Above *Clown fish are able to nestle among the stinging tentacles of anemones without getting stung. They lay their eggs at the base of anemones, so they too are protected from hungry fish.*

Left *A beautiful Australian jellyfish shelters a fish from attackers.*

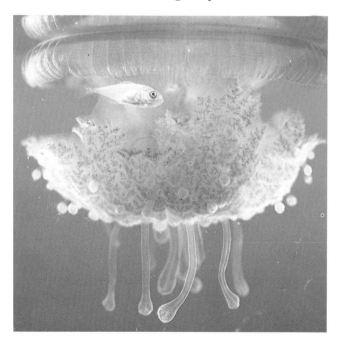

sometimes feeds on scraps of food left over by the anemone and will chase away fish trying to eat the anemone.

Some hermit crabs like to have sea anemones on their shells because the stinging cells of the anemone may help protect the crab from attackers such as fish. The sea anemone may climb on the hermit crab's shell by itself, or the hermit crab may pick up the anemone gently in its pincers and place it on its shell. In return for protecting the hermit crab, the sea anemone gets scraps of food and a mobile home.

As a hermit crab grows, it usually has to find a bigger shell to live in. Some hermit crabs use sea anemones to form an extension to their shells; this saves them from having to look for a new home. The anemones they use are called cloak anemones.

The sea fir also grows on a hermit crab's shell, which is as good a place to

Giving a ride to a sea anemone is a good way for a hermit crab to protect itself. An attacker, such as an octopus, will be driven away by the anemone's stings. The sea anemone feeds on the crab's leftovers.

grow as any rock surface. The stinging tentacles protect the hermit crab, while the sea fir feeds on the hermit crab's leftovers.

Enemies

In spite of having stinging tentacles, jellyfish and their close relatives are eaten by certain animals that are not affected by their stings. Jellyfish are

This sea slug likes to eat a variety of stinging creatures, including this porpita.

eaten by some fish, and they are the favorite food of some turtles.

Sea anemones are attacked by sea

spiders, which suck out their juices. Sea slugs also eat sea anemones, as well as sea firs. They like to nibble at the tentacles. Surprisingly, sea slugs are able to eat the stinging cells without causing them to fire. The stings are then passed to pouches on the sea slug's back, thus protecting it from hungry fish.

Even the venomous Portuguese man-of-war is eaten by some animals. A sea slug steals the stings to use as its own weapon. Sea snails, turtles and fish also feast on the Portuguese man-of-war.

You would not think corals are worth eating because of their hard skeleton. But some animals do manage to eat them. Parrot fish have tough teeth, so they can scrape off bits of coral and grind it up to extract the goodness. Crown-of-thorns starfish push out their stomachs to digest the fleshy parts of coral.

Beadlet anemones will sometimes fight each other to gain more living space.

Sometimes sea anemones fight each other for space on a rock. Their weapons are patches of stinging cells that swell up on the side facing the other anemone. They rear up and slowly bash each other with these stinging patches. The loser either creeps away or detaches itself from the rock and floats off. If an anemone cannot escape it may be killed. Battles occur only between anemones that belong to different families.

4
Reproduction

A hydra with a new bud on its side.

Budding

Sea anemones and corals can reproduce themselves by splitting in two or more parts. This is called **budding**. Some sea anemones inch along the surface of a rock leaving behind small parts of the base, which grow into new anemones. Other kinds of anemones split in two. All corals start out life on a rock as a single polyp. If conditions are good, colonial corals then produce more and more polyps by budding.

Hydras, which live in freshwater ponds and streams, reproduce by budding in the warmer months. A bud forms on the side of the hydra. After several days the bud grows tentacles and detaches from its parent. It then settles on a surface of a stone or twig, and fends for itself.

In colder times of the year the hydra produces **eggs**. These are

formed on the side of the parent's body. After the egg is **fertilized**, a little hydra develops inside. But the egg may hatch only when the weather becomes warmer.

The snakelocks sea anemone shown above is reproducing itself by splitting in two. This is called budding. Each new part will grow into an individual snakelocks anemone.

Life Cycles

Jellyfish and their relatives go through different stages during their lives. Such changes are called life cycles. During its feeding stage the jellyfish is a bell-shaped medusa. Jellyfish medusas shed **sperm** and eggs into the sea. Once an egg is fertilized by a sperm, it develops into a swimming **larva**, which settles on the bottom of the sea and grows into a little polyp. The polyp then buds off lots of little medusas, which grow up into jellyfish.

During its feeding stage the sea fir is a colony of polyps. Some of these polyps bud off medusas that are like tiny jellyfish. These medusas shed sperm and eggs into the sea. The fertilized egg develops into a swimming larva, which settles on

This illustration shows all the different stages in the life cycle of a jellyfish.

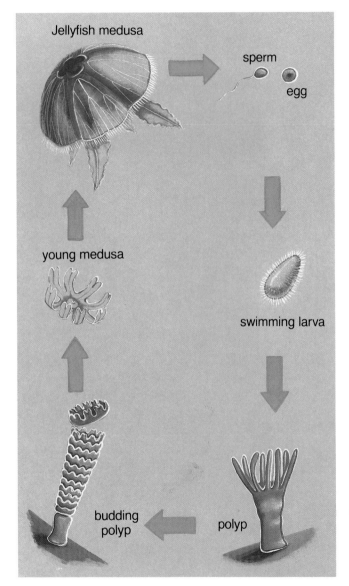

Jellyfish medusa

sperm

egg

young medusa

swimming larva

budding polyp

polyp

the bottom and grows into a new sea fir.

Sea anemones can also produce young inside their bodies. The sperm enters the sea anemone's body opening and fertilizes an egg. The fertilized egg develops inside the sea anemone and the larva emerges from the anemone's mouth.

Corals shed sperm and eggs into the water. The fertilized egg develops into a swimming larva, settles down on the bottom and grows into a new coral polyp. Recently, scientists have discovered that many different kinds of corals on Australia's Great Barrier Reef shed their eggs and sperm all on the same night in the year. So many eggs and sperm are produced that it looks like an underwater snowstorm. One reason for spawning on the same night may be so that fish feeding on the eggs will soon have their fill and most of the eggs will be spared. Or it

A brain coral sheds bundles of eggs and sperm. The bundles will break open to release the eggs and sperm. The fertilized eggs develop into larvae, which settle on the seabed and grow into new coral polyps.

may be that the corals all reproduce on the night of the year that provides as long a period of calm water between the tides as possible. This would give the sperm plenty of time to fertilize the eggs before the currents sweep them away.

5
Jellyfish, Corals and People

It is much better to photograph coral than to collect it for souvenirs.

Dangerous Jellyfish

The stings of jellyfish can be painful. You should be careful not to swim near jellyfish or pick one up on the beach since it might have a powerful sting. Jellyfish are often given names like "sea nettle" to show that they sting. The most dangerous jellyfish are the sea wasps, which live in the warm waters of the Pacific Ocean. These jellyfish have killed several people off the coast of Australia. Death usually occurs between three and twenty minutes after being stung. Even small stings by sea wasps can cause deep wounds.

The Portuguese man-of-war, which lives in warm waters, is also feared by people, although its stings are not as dangerous as those of a sea wasp. If you touched one of the long trailing tentacles of a Portuguese man-of-war, the pain would shoot up your arm. A small sting lasts only a few hours, but a strong sting can last several weeks. Where stinging jellyfish are washed inshore, people may be warned not to go swimming.

Some kinds of sea anemones and sea firs can also inflict nasty stings.

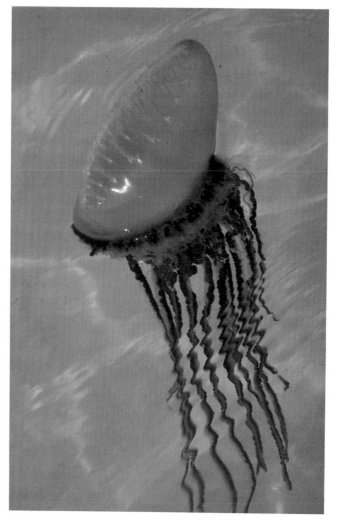

Above left *Sea nettles can inflict sharp stings. If they appear inshore, swimmers do not stay in the water.*

Above right *A sting from the Portuguese man-of-war can be extremely painful.*

Beautiful Corals

A coral reef off the coast of Bermuda. A variety of soft and hard corals grow here.

Living corals are among the most beautiful sights in the world. In some places, corals have been killed by mistake when buildings were constructed next to the sea. The waste building materials that were thrown into the sea made the seawater murky and, therefore, killed off the corals. Chemicals used to kill weeds may wash into the sea and damage corals. Sometimes fishermen have killed coral by blowing up or smashing parts of reefs to get at valuable fish and shellfish. Anchoring boats on reefs can also cause damage to the sensitive corals.

There are now underwater reserves where corals are protected. People can visit these reserves and look at the corals, but they are not allowed to fish or damage the living corals.

People collect bits of dead coral because it looks pretty. Souvenirs made from coral are popular throughout the world. If these are made from pieces of coral that have already died, no harm is done to beautiful living coral.

Some kinds of coral are polished to

A collection of corals on sale in the Philippines. Reefs are damaged when pieces are broken off as souvenirs.

make jewelry. The most popular coral is red coral, which is the inner skeleton of a soft coral. This is collected in the Mediterranean Sea and off the coast of Japan.

6
Learning More

A cannonball jellyfish washed ashore. Some stranded jellyfish may survive if quickly washed out to sea again.

On the Seashore

The safest place to see jellyfish and their relatives is on the seashore. You should go looking when the tide is going out. Jellyfish are often found washed up after a storm, or you may find them trapped in a rockpool. Remember not to pick them up because they may sting.

Sea anemones are found in damp places on shore, either in rockpools or under rocks. A rockpool is like your own aquarium. See if you can find out what sea anemones like to eat. Offer them a shrimp, if you have a net to catch one. See if your anemone retracts (pulls in) its tentacles if you gently prod it with a pencil. Some anemones retract their tentacles, others do not.

If you place a see-through plastic container on the surface of a rockpool you can see what is happening more

Above left *This common jellyfish is floating above green seaweed. Its eggs are produced in the purple rings.*

Above right *Giant green anemones live in rockpools along the Pacific coast of the United States. Starfish also like rockpools.*

easily. For smaller animals, such as sea firs, you will need a magnifying glass to see them properly. See if there are different kinds of anemones in your

pool. You could draw them using colored pencils and then find out what kind they are by looking in a guide book of seashore animals.

Under Water

Jellyfish and their relatives look much better under water. If you can swim well, you might learn how to use a mask and snorkel. The mask keeps water out of your eyes and has a glass front so that you can see clearly under water. The snorkel is a short tube that stays above the surface of the water to allow you to breathe while you are swimming under water. Snorkeling can be dangerous, so you

These colorful jewel anemones are found on rocks under water.

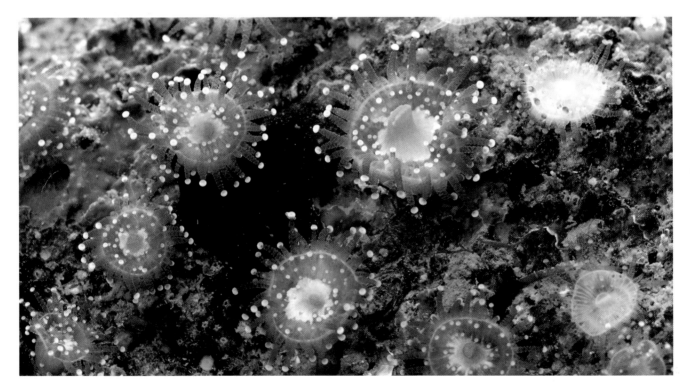

must be taught how to use the equipment safely.

Never swim close to jellyfish; you might get stung. And remember, some have long, thin tentacles that trail behind them, so be sure to give them lots of room. It is fun to float above sea anemones, watching to see if they catch any food.

In the tropics you can snorkel over a coral reef. If you want to see coral reefs without getting wet, you can take a trip in a glass-bottomed boat.

Another way to see marine life is to visit an aquarium. Corals are very hard to keep alive in aquariums. Most displays of coral fish do not have living corals. Sea anemones are easier to keep alive in aquariums.

If you want to study sea anemones closely, you can set up your own aquarium. You will need a strong glass tank and a pump to blow air into the seawater. You may need permission

Jellyfish look their best under water, like this one photographed in the Great Barrier Reef, Australia.

to collect anemones from the seashore. In case the anemones you find have harmful stings, wear waterproof gloves to protect your hands. You should take only a few animals to study. When you have finished looking at them, you should put them back where you found them so that there will be plenty of anemones for other people to look at.

Glossary

Algae Microscopic one-celled plants and seaweeds.

Atoll A ring-like coral reef with a lagoon in the center.

Budding Formation of a new individual from a growth on the body of the parent.

Cilia Fine hair-like parts growing out of some animal and plant cells.

Coelenterates A group of animals including jellyfish, sea anemones and corals that have a hollow gut with only one opening.

Colony Among corals and their relatives, a colony refers to a group of individuals that are joined together and work together.

Egg The reproductive cell produced by the female.

Evolved Developed gradually over time – to adapt to changing conditions.

Fertilized An egg is fertilized when it is joined with a sperm. When fertilized, the egg develops into a new individual.

Fossils Impressions or remains of living organisms preserved in old rocks.

Larva (plural, larvae) The young form of certain animals, such as an insect or a jellyfish, before it changes into its adult form.

Medusa Bell-shaped stage in the life cycle of a jellyfish and its relatives during which it swims freely in the sea.

Plankton Small animals and plants that float or drift in seas and lakes.

Polyp Stage in the life cycle of a jellyfish and its relatives during which it is stuck onto a surface. Sea anemones are polyps.

Prey An animal hunted or caught for food.

Sperm The reproductive cell produced by the male.

Spicules Needle-like pieces of hard material that help support soft tissues.

Volcano A mountain with an opening through which very hot melted rock comes up, or has come up in the past, from a crack in the earth's crust.

Finding Out More

To find out more about jellyfish, sea anemones and corals, you can read the following books:

Oxford Scientific. *Jellyfish & Other Sea Creatures* Putnam Publishing Group, 1982

Philip Steele. *Life in the Sea* Warwick Press, 1986

John F. Waters. *A Jellyfish is Not a Fish.* Crowell Jr. Books, 1979

Picture Acknowledgments

All photographs are from Oxford Scientific Films by the following photographers: Doug Allan 11 (top); Katie Atkinson 18; G.I. Bernard 11 (bottom), 12, 20, 23, 24, 27 (right), 42; Waina Cheng 41 (left); John Cheverton 33; John A. Cooke 25, 32; Jack Dermid 40; Fredrik Ehrenstrom *cover*, 14, 15, 19 (left), 36; M.P.L. Fogden 41 (right); Laurence Gould 9 (right), 36, 38; Peter Harrison 35; Rodger Jackman 29, 31; Breck P. Kent 16; Rudie H. Kuiter 9 (left); Zig Leszczynski 37 (left); Miranda MacQuitty 39; Peter Parks *frontispiece*, 8, 13 (top), 17, 19 (right), 26, 27 (left), 28 (left), 30, 37 (right), 43; Kjell B. Sandved 21; David Shale 28 (right); Len Zell 22. The illustrations on pages 10, 25 and 34 were supplied by Jackie Harland.

Index

The numbers in **bold** refer to the pictures

a39092 02353 9093b

WHITE MOUNTAIN LIBRARY
Sweetwater County Library System
Rock Springs, Wyoming

WHITE MOUNTAIN LIBRARY
2935 SWEETWATER DRIVE
ROCK SPRINGS, WY   82901

WM J 593.7 Mac 11.90
39092023539093
MacQuitty, Miranda.
Discovering jellyfish